PEARLS OF WISDOM

for business and life

by
Roger L. Kirkham

Acknowlegdments

My thanks to Clark Chamberlain, Illustrator.

My thanks to the following who provided valuable additions and improvements to the pearls: Merlene Swenson, Alma Allred, Keith Poelman, COL Stephen J. Oren USMC, Ernie Wessman, Douglas Duehlmeier, Gary Farber, Dave Allred, Yvette Bernatene, Eduardo Andrade, Emma Kemp, Brian McGavin, Arnold Wagner, Bob Secondo, Luke Smith, Eileen Longsworth, Dwayne Liddell, and Jack Woodall.

My thanks to Judy Ann, who is the pearl of my life, for providing unending encouragement.

First Printing, August 1994

Copyright © 1994
Crystal Publishing, Inc.
All rights reserved. No part of this work may be reproduced or transmitted in any form without express written permission of the publisher.

Crystal Publishing, Inc., Publisher
Roger L. Kirkham, Author & Editor

Crystal Publishing, Inc.
P.O. Box 526145
Salt Lake City, Utah
84152-6145

ISBN 1-880184-40-0

PEARL: a gem of fine quality

WISDOM: insightful knowledge
and good judgment,
based on experience.

**This book contains pearls
of wisdom on:**

- Problem Solving
- Influencing Without Authority
- Improvement
- Managing Change
- Effective Leadership
- Customer Service
- Quality
- Controlling Quality and Service

Each pearl of wisdom is a valuable lesson or food for thought condensed into an easily readable format.

Each pearl and its discussion stands alone in under standability, and complements the other pearls in its topic area.

This book is based on twenty years experience in management, communication, and continuous improvement training and consulting.

Keep the "Pearls" handy to unlock needed insight for continuous improvement, for help with problems, or just for a daily recharge.

Table of Contents

Problem Solving 1
    People who want milk 2
    Fixing a problem 3
    Failing to confront fear 5
    Failure is never permanent 6
    The last of the human freedoms 7
    You can do nothing about the past 9
    Avoid blaming 10
    Obtaining admission of guilt 11
    Your reaction 12
    Owning a problem 14
    Most people own more problems. 15
    Those who never accept ownership 16
    You can't have vital experience 17
    To help without owning 18
    Effective listening. 19
    I can hardly wait 21
    Separate the vital few 22

Influencing Without Authority 23
    Influencing 24
    To influence others 25
    Choose to change your perceptions 26
    How you say something 27
    People respond to their perceptions. 29
    Improving your influence 30
    How well you communicate 31
    Winning means losing 33
    Getting the response 34

The message received 35
People's thinking 36
Clear writing 37
Clear thinking 38
Start with the most important thing 39
Keep It Short & Simple 41
Opinions influence 42
Complainers. 43
Dumping data 45
People may not care 46
The decision maker's perception 47
To overcome indifference 48
To get action 49
To win support 50
To overcome a "no,". 51
Never exaggerate 52
Minimum expectations 53

Improvement 54
Security and stability 55
Improvement always 57
Change never guarantees improvement 58
Reorganizing improves nothing 59
Getting in the groove 60
We have met the enemy 62
All improvement 63
Treat attitude 64
Focus improvement 65
If you stay the same 67
To focus improvement 68
Do or do not. 69

No *instant* pudding 72
Change always costs 73
Improvement always pays 74

Managing Change 75
Back to the good-old-days 77
The goal of changing 78
We must be the change 79
Change by compliance 81
Change by commitment 82
Start small 83
People resist change 84
Minimize uncertainty 85
Use what you learn 87

Effective Leadership 88
Effective leaders 89
Traditional management 91
Authority 92
The most valuable skill 93
Effective leaders *enable* 94
Using authority influences 95
Malicious compliance 96
Empowering 97
Knowing the right question 99
To get commitment to change 100
Clearly define your target 101
Goals + pain or gain 103
Effectiveness 104
Everyone in the same direction 105
Meetings focus on effectiveness 106

People respond 107
To be accountable 108

Customer Service 109
The only purpose for any job 111
Meaningful feedback 112
Your best is not good enough 113
Your enemy may be your customer 114
Keeping your eye on the goal 115
To delight customers 117
Being busy 119
Avoid this assumption 120
The customer is not always right 121
Thinking shuts down 123
Pay particular attention 124

Quality 125
Join the Quality Revolution 127
Simple definition: Quality 128
More sophisticated definition 129
Dangerously wrong definition 130
Quality of work determines 131
You will never be better 132
The quality of suppliers' work 133
Total Quality 134

Controlling Quality and Service 135
Out of control 136
No complaints mean nothing 137
After-the-fact measurements 139
Authority does not control 140

Controlling Quality and Service 135
No feedback means out of control 136
No complaints mean nothing 137
After-the-fact measurements do not control quality ... 139
Authority does not control quality or service 140
Inspection of output does not ensure future quality ... 141
Just because your numbers look good, does not mean
        quality and service are in control 143
The drive-in-window approach gives no lasting
        improvement 144
To maintain quality and service, control the work
        process 145
If you cannot define it, you cannot control it 146
To focus control, define quality in terms of quality
        characteristics 147
Controlling one quality characteristic does not
        ensure control of the others 148
Each quality characteristic requires its own work
        system 149
Sufficiently controlling the quality of work
        guarantees quality of output 150
The 5 Evils measure process performance 151

About The Author

Roger L. Kirkham is president of the American Training Alliance, specializing in continuous improvement training and consulting. Over the past twenty years, Mr. Kirkham has provided management and communication training for thousands of participants for clients in government, industry, and business.

He is author of the book *A Better Way: Achieving Total Quality* and has produced a four cassette, audio seminar, *Total Quality in Government, Industry & Business*. He is a licensed professional engineer and teaches part time at the University of Utah.

Mr. Kirkham is the proud father of five children, loves snow skiing and fishing in Utah, has climbed the Grand Teton in Wyoming and Mt. Fuji in Japan, and is sure that the smartest thing he ever did was marry Judy Ann Gowans.

American Training Alliance
P.O. Box 9482
Salt Lake City, UT 84109-0482
(801)521-9267; FAX (801)278-7685

Problem Solving

**Some people want to arrive
without making the trip.**

> ## "People who want milk should not seat themselves on a stool in the middle of a field in the hope that a cow will back up to them." - Elbert Hubbard

You have three options when confronted with a problem:

1. *Suffer*: do nothing except wish that things would change and hope that somehow things will get better.
2. *Get Out*: quit, leave, transfer, or hope the person causing you problems dies, retires, or moves to a different continent.
3. *Confront*: confront the problem and seek a solution.

A surprising number of people choose option #1.

Problem Solving

Fixing a problem does not necessarily prevent it from happening again.

Fixing a flat tire enables you to return to normal travel. But what if you got a flat tire every day? Daily fixing the flat tire would not prevent flat tires from recurring.

Similarly, correcting one misspelled word does not necessarily prevent other misspelled words.

Fixing a problem returns you to normal operation, but does not improve future operations.

Improving operations requires changing the way something is done.

Failing to confront fear of the unknown means living a life of quiet desperation.

Problem Solving

Failing to confront fear of the unknown means living a life of quiet desperation.

Tragedy is suffering in vain. Suffering in vain comes from failing to confront fear of the unknown:

"I've been here 17 years now and have had six months experience repeated *thirty-four* times...."

"—Why haven't you looked for something else before now?"

"...I don't know...."

OR

"I've been living in hell for the past seven years...."

"—Why didn't you seek help before now?"

"...I don't know...."

Overcoming this useless suffering requires making a change.

Problem Solving

Failure is never permanent, unless you let it be.

People only fail when they give up. Falling down is not failure. Not getting back up again is failure. Mistakes can be a great, future time saver—we know what not to do next time. If you tried one thing and it did not work, try something different.

After 10 years of failing to win any medals in seven races over four Olympics, finally at his last chance, Dan Jansen won his first gold medal — his first Olympic medal of any kind — with a world record in the men's 1,000 meter speed skating race at the 1994 Winter Olympics.

Not experiencing failure means no one is trying anything different. Nothing different means no improvement. No improvement can prove to be permanent failure.

Problem Solving

"...the last of the human freedoms: to choose one's attitude in any given set of circumstances...."

"We who lived in [Nazi] concentration camps can remember the men who walked through the huts comforting others, giving away their last piece of bread. They may have been few in number, but they offer sufficient proof that everything can be taken from a man but one thing: the last of the human freedoms - to choose one's attitude in any given set of circumstances, to choose one's own way...The experiences of camp life show that man does have a choice of action. There were enough examples, often of a heroic nature, which proved that apathy could be overcome, irritability suppressed... Fundamentally, therefore, any man can, even under such circumstances, decide what shall become of him - mentally and spiritually. He may retain his human dignity even in a concentration camp." Man's Search for Meaning, Viktor E. Frankl, Touchstone Book, 1962, pp. 65-66.

You can do nothing about the past—
but you can learn from it.

Problem Solving

You can do nothing about the past— but you can learn from it.

Worrying about what might have been, what could have been, if only... drains emotion and time; it locks us in the past. Nothing can be done about the past. However, the past can be a great teacher—if we learn from it.

Past problems can be guideposts to future success. We blind ourselves to opportunities for improvement by never climbing out of the ruts of the past. If we are not careful, our ruts can become our graves.

Wisdom is learning from others' past mistakes, instead of having to learn from our own.

Problem Solving

Avoid blaming and embrace planning for future improvement.

Blame mires people in the past. Blaming condemns someone for an existing problem. Blaming discourages, inhibits, undermines, obstructs, and constrains. Blame institutes a WIN-LOSE frame of mind by concentrating on shame and guilt for whoever caused the problem. Assigning blame improves nothing. Instead, blaming encourages lying and deceit—"Don't get caught again."

Future improvement requires changes made today. Planning brings the future into the present so you can do something about it now!

Planning for improvement establishes a WIN-WIN frame of mind by concentrating on changes to solve current problems and to prevent future problems.

Problem Solving

Obtaining admission of guilt does not resolve problems.

People suffering from problems they did not cause sometimes try to switch from LOSE-WIN to WIN-LOSE. They want those causing the problem to admit guilt, thus motivating them to change the error of their ways....

Most people, however, react defensively when confronted and quickly switch from defense to offense resulting in LOSE-LOSE: everybody loses.

Nothing is improved by admitting guilt unless something changes. To achieve improvement, concentrate on what needs to change instead of who needs to change. Although you cannot change people's personalities, you can get them to change what they are doing and how they are doing it, which is WIN-WIN.

Problem Solving

You choose your reaction to your problems.

There was a man who took his lunch every day in a lunch pail to work. One day he opened his lunch pail, unwrapped his sandwich, took one bite and exclaimed, "Oh, no! A peanut butter sandwich!" He then threw the sandwich on the ground and stomped on it. That got everybody's attention.

He took out another sandwich and took a bite out of it. "I can't believe it! Another peanut butter sandwich!" He threw that one down and stomped on it.

He took out one more sandwich. Everyone could hardly wait to see how he would react this time. As he unwrapped the sandwich, he said through clenched teeth, "This better not be another peanut butter sandwich!" ☞

Problem Solving

—continued from previous page

One of his buddies sitting by him had become quite concerned and remarked, "Wait a minute. We can't all have roast beef for lunch everyday. We all live on limited budgets. Your wife is doing the best she can."

"Leave my wife out of this," the man snapped back. "—I pack my own lunch!"

Moral of the story: Unlike the man in this story, we cannot always choose our circumstances or our problems. However, we are response-*able*. We are able to choose how we react to those problems.

Problem Solving

Owning a problem does not mean you caused the problem.

Causing a problem has nothing to do with who owns a problem.
Whoever chooses to resolve a problem assumes problem ownership.

Experiencing a problem is not the same as owning a problem. In fact,
whoever caused a problem may expend great effort in *not* owning the
problem.

If something is unacceptable to you (you are bothered, frustrated,
deprived, needful, or disturbed), and you determine to resolve the
problem, you take ownership of the problem—even if you did not cause
the problem.

Problem Solving

Most people own more problems than necessary.

Offering suggestions, giving advice, telling someone how to solve their problem gives problem ownership to you.

Trying to influence another person with facts, logic, counter-arguments, or your own opinion, transfers problem ownership to you. Instructing someone on what to do and how to do it confers problem ownership upon you.

Owning someone else's problem is not wrong, but it usually is not what the other person needs most. Parents and supervisors seem particularly prone to owning more problems than is helpful.

"A hard thing about business is minding your own." *The Road To Success*, Larry Wall and Kathleen Russell, Walrus Productions, p. 21

Problem Solving

Those who never accept ownership of their problems, never learn to solve problems.

As children, some people coped with their problems using tears or anger to intimidate others into taking over their problems—and carried those manipulative habits into adulthood.

This behavior prevents individuals from learning to solve their own problems. For example:
- if the solutions they receive are good, the next time problems arise, they must return to their source for the *right* answers;
- if the solutions they receive do not work, then it is always someone else's fault. They feel no responsibility for someone else's failed solutions.

Problem Solving

"You can't have vital experience without having it." - Truman Madsen

You cannot know what salt tastes like until you taste salt. You cannot learn to swim without swimming. You cannot describe the color blue if you have never seen the color blue. You cannot know what raising children is like until you raise your own.

Some things must be experienced to be understood or mastered.

You cannot learn to solve problems until you have to solve your own problems *and* live with the consequences.

Problem Solving

To help without owning the problem, listen to understand.

Some people spend large sums of money to find someone who knows how to listen to understand.

Listening to understand helps the person with the problem gain perspective. It is like holding up a mirror for the other person to take a closer look.

If you do not think receiving feedback is helpful, try not looking in a mirror for a week.

Listening to understand is one of the most caring human responses. Friends listen to understand.

Problem Solving

Effective listening requires suspending judgment.

Judging prevents understanding. Our educational process teaches us to be analytical and critical, which can get in the way of listening to understand.

Suspending judgment means you do not listen to agree or disagree, to like or dislike what is said. Suspending judgment means you do not interpret other people's motives nor blame them for their problems. Suspending judgment means you do not try to talk people out of their feelings or try to make the feelings go away.

Listening to understand means concentrating on the other's point of view. Reflecting back your understanding of what is said, demonstrates that you understand and helps the other person clarify the problem.

"I can hardly wait to hear what I'm going to say next."

Problem Solving

"I can hardly wait to hear what I'm going to say next."

Have you ever tried to share a problem with people and they start finishing your sentences for you? Then they move on to apparently more important things—*what they want to say*.

Instead of listening, most people spend their listening time preparing what they are going to say next.

Effective listening usually does not depend on hearing the other person as much as concentrating on understanding the other person's perspective and point of view.

"Seek first to understand, then be understood." - Stephen R. Covey

Problem Solving

"Separate the vital few from the trivial many." - Joseph Juran

Most of the effect comes from a small portion of the causes.
For example:
- 80% of the problems come from 20% of the possible causes.
- 80% of the interruptions come from 20% of the people interrupting.
- 80% of the complaints come from 20% of the customers.
- 80% of the significant results are achieved by 20% of the people.
- 80% of the cost is in 20% of the inventory.

To be effective *and* efficient, separate the vital few from the trivial many. Concentrate your efforts where it matters most.

Influencing Without Authority

Influence by: persuading, convincing, impelling, swaying, inspiring, motivating.

Influencing without authority is the ability to make good things happen without using force.

Influencing Without Authority

Influencing should never equate with manipulating.

Do you manipulate or do you influence? Manipulation is achieving your own outcome at the expense of or without regard for someone else. Manipulation is WIN-LOSE.

Manipulation generates so much resentment that the people you want to influence the most will not deal with you. Two manipulators people often use:
- tears,
- anger.

Influencing is achieving your outcome while helping others to also achieve theirs, or at least not interfere with theirs. Influencing should be WIN-WIN.

Influencing Without Authority

To influence others *more* effectively, you must first change your perception of them.

Your biased, narrow, subjective, prejudiced perceptions of people virtually automatically program how you influence them, because perceptions determine:
- how you feel,
- how you communicate, and
- how you behave.

Therefore, if you do not first change your perception of the person you want to influence, trying harder will probably just reinforce your preconceived feelings, communication, and behavior.

Influencing Without Authority

Choose to change your perceptions.

Consider two perceptions of a typical teenager:

- rebellious
- moody
- irresponsible   OR
- selfish
- lazy
- immature

- pressured
- lonely
- very self-conscious
- often feels
  overwhelmed
- feels ugly

Both sets of perceptions are of the same teenager. Would it make much difference which set of perceptions were chosen in interacting with this teenager?

Changing your perception of others does not guarantee they will improve. But you will improve.

Influencing Without Authority

How you say something influences more than *what* you say.

Your tone of voice, raised eyebrows, rolling your eyes, a shrug of your shoulders can speak volumes more than what you say.

Your perception of the person to whom you are communicating virtually locks in *how* you communicate.

How we judge others packages our perceptions of them. To change how you influence others, you must first suspend judgment and *seek to understand them*. Then, speak to be understood.

People respond to their perceptions in spite of reality.

Influencing Without Authority

People respond to their perceptions in spite of reality.

To speak to be understood, you must be sensitive to the perceptions of the person you want to influence.

People filter others' communication through their own one-sided, limited, preconceived perceptions.

To influence others, first listen to understand their perspective or point of view.

You do not have to agree or disagree, like or dislike their perspective. Just try to understand it. This suspends judgment on your part and enables you to speak to be understood.

Influencing Without Authority

Improving your influence increases your value to an organization.

Individuals are of infinite worth in terms of human value. However, your organizational value is finite and is determined by your ability to contribute to achieving the organization's mission.

There is only so much you can do individually on any given day. Increasing your value to an organization does not mean working harder or putting in more time. Rather, it means improving your ability to influence others.

Influencing others to improve continuously greatly increases your value to an organization. Organizations need clear thinking that enables continuous improvement of work processes.

Influencing Without Authority

How well you communicate determines how much influence you have.

Personally and professionally, our relationships with others determine the quality of our living. How well we communicate determines how well we interrelate with others and how much influence we have.

People do not care how smart you are if they cannot *benefit* from how smart you are.

We do not lack for great ideas. We lack for great ideas that are under stood and put to use. How well ideas are communicated determines how well they are understood and used.

Winning means losing, if you're dead right.

Influencing Without Authority

Winning means losing, if you are *dead* right.

"Dead right" means you may be right, but nobody cares. Your influence is dead. Therefore, you lose, even though you may be "right."

If the only way you can be right is for someone else to be wrong, if the only way for you to win is for someone else to lose, you will have little influence.

> Here lies John Jay,
> Who died maintaining his right of way.
> He was right, dead right, as he sped along,
> But he's just as dead as if he were wrong.

There is no future in being dead right.

Influencing Without Authority

Effective communication means getting the response you want.

It is easy to know how effective you are in communicating. Ask yourself: "What response do I want?"
If you get the response you want, you are effective.

When you make a phone call, exactly what response do you want? What do you want the other person to do or say? When you write a letter or memo, precisely what do you want the other person to do and when do you want him or her to do it?

The more precisely, directly, and to the point you can identify your desired response, the more effective your communication is.

Influencing Without Authority

The message received determines the response you get.

The message you *thought* you sent may not be the one actually received because of misunderstandings, skepticism, or inexperience of the person receiving your communication.

Whatever message is received is the one that influences.

Misunderstandings are difficult to get past because you must overcome the influence of the wrong message before the right message gets through.

If you do not get the response you want, deliver the message a different way.

Influencing Without Authority

People's thinking is an organization's most valuable resource.

Any organization has seven resources to get the job done:
- people
- money
- time
- materials
- facilities
- equipment
- information

Of these resources, people are the most important. People determine the use of all the other resources.

The one ability people have which makes them more valuable than the other resources is the ability to *think*.

Influencing Without Authority

Clear writing forces clear thinking.

Writing focuses thinking. Writing also forces editing of thinking for content, understandability, and relevancy.

Incorrect grammar or misspelled words greatly distract from the message and therefore, dilute influence. However, meticulously correct grammar and spelling do not compensate for muddy thinking.

It is the thinking conveyed in writing that influences.

Clear thinking becomes clear writing. One cannot exist without the other.

Influencing Without Authority

Clear thinking enables clear communication.

No one has time to play, "Guess what I'm thinking" when others are not clear in communicating. How much others benefit from your thinking depends on how clearly you communicate.

Each day we face information overload. We have an overabundance of data. Information is no substitute for thinking. The more information we have to convey, the more competent and concise our thinking must be.

Clear thinking enables clear communication, which is crucial for influencing without authority.

Influencing Without Authority

Start with the most important thing.

When trying to influence, start with the most important thing which:
- captures attention,
- immediately orients the receiver to what is most important, and
- enables all subsequent discussion to reinforce what is most important.

To decide what is the most important thing to say or write, ask:
"What message, if accurately understood and responded to, will give me the desired response?"

The message that will give you your desired response is the most important thing.

K.I.S.S.: Keep It Short & Simple

Influencing Without Authority

K.I.S.S.: Keep It Short & Simple

While the study of literature teaches style, vocabulary and how to paint word pictures, traditional English classes do not focus on how to get a specific response from communication.

In business, keep it short and get to the point!

If you do not get the response you want, it does not matter how fancy your words were or how smooth and flowing your style was. It takes no talent to make things complicated.

To get the response you want, keep it simple. Use language, examples, and terminology familiar to the receiver.

Influencing Without Authority

Opinions influence more than facts.

The higher a person rises in an organization, the more responsibility and authority a person has, the more this person is paid for his or her opinions.

Opinions are not more important than facts. Opinions without facts to back them up lose credibility. The point is: opinions *influence* more than facts.

This is because:
1. humans do not effectively process large streams of new data and information,
2. organizations rely on the thinking of their most valuable resource - people. People's thinking is based on their judgment, conclusions, experience and education—in other words, their opinions.

Influencing Without Authority

Complainers, even if they are right, have little influence.

Complainers are usually perceived negatively. Complainers seem to whine and moan about how bad things are and how good things could be if everything were different.

Reinforcing existing problems, although increasing pain and getting people's attention, does not make problems easier to solve. In fact, complaining may drive people away from dealing with problems.

Problem solvers are perceived positively and have a lot of influence. To be a problem solver, recognize the need for change and identify positive solutions to achieve that improvement.

Dumping data does not deliver a message.

Influencing Without Authority

Dumping data does not deliver a message.

If you dump data but deliver no message, people may be impressed with how busy you were, but you will have little influence.

You should have a reason for providing facts and data. Facts and data should be used to support and back up the message you want to deliver but not as a substitute for the message.

Opinions and conclusions should contain the message you want to deliver.

The message received from facts and data is what will influence.

Influencing Without Authority

People may not care *what* you want until they understand *why*.

Too often we expect others to respond to our requests simply because we make the request. However, people resist or ignore requests they perceive are unreasonable.

Understanding *why* something is wanted provides a reason, which helps make a request reasonable. People respond to requests they perceive are reasonable.

People do not have to like your reason, but they must understand it.

To aid in understanding, it helps if people know in some detail how you will use what you request from them. Encourage them to visit you and see how you use what they provide.

Influencing Without Authority

The decision maker's perception is the only one that counts.

There are good reasons for decision makers sometimes seeming skeptical, negative or indifferent to suggestions and proposals. Decision makers are *personally* accountable for what results from suggestions and proposals they approve.

If you are deeply concerned about something the decision maker perceives is trivial, then, your suggestions will be trivial to the decision maker.

To establish the significance of your suggestions and proposals, emphasize the urgency of the problems by answering these two questions:
   1) "Why should this be considered now?"
   2) "What if nothing is done?"

Influencing Without Authority

To overcome indifference, clarify:
"Why should this be considered *now*?"

To get people to pay attention to proposals, requests, suggestions or
recommendations, they must first understand:
- What is the sense of urgency?
- Why is what you want more important than what is already
  planned?
- Why have you not brought this up before now?
- What is the significance of the problem you propose to resolve?

If the people you want to influence see no urgency to consider what you
want *now*, they probably will not consider it. They will think they have
more important things to do.

Influencing Without Authority

To get action, clarify: "What if nothing is done?"

To convince people to take action, they must recognize the *future* implications of doing nothing.

Emphasize what the cost and impact will be of staying the same:
- whether current problems will stay the same or get worse,
- what will be the cost if current problems stay the same,
- what will be the cost if current problems get worse,
- how many new problems will arise,
- what will be the cost of each new problem,
- how long the impact of each new problem will be felt.

Influencing Without Authority

To win support for your ideas, reduce risk for the decision maker.

People who make decisions are ultimately accountable for those decisions, and no one likes to take all the risk and to have all the accountability.

To minimize risk, decision makers will either say no or decide not to decide. Overcome indecision by establishing the urgency and significance of the problem.

To overcome a "no" you must emphasize the benefits so convincingly that the decision maker cannot refuse your ideas.

Influencing Without Authority

To overcome a "no," *EMPHASIZE* the benefits.

Simply conveying information does not provide any **emphasis**.

To get support for your ideas, suggestions and recommendations, you must *EMPHASIZE* the benefits or improvement from your ideas, suggestions, and recommendations. For example:
- How many things will improve?
- How much improvement will there be as indicated by what?
- How soon will improvement come?
- How long will improvement last?
- How much will the improvement cost and how does that compare with the benefits measured over the life cycle of the improvements?

Influencing Without Authority

Never exaggerate when trying to influence others.

You can really get people's attention by exaggerating. For example: make the problem sound bigger than it really is and promise unbelievable amounts of improvement.

You will also lose your credibility by exaggerating.
No credibility = no trust = no influence!

Even if your ideas are good, even if your recommendations will work, even if improvement is guaranteed, you will never be listened to if you have no credibility. Loss of trust extends far into the future.

Small successes establish good credibility. It takes much more effort to overcome loss of trust than it does to establish good credibility.

Influencing Without Authority

People usually respond to *minimum* expectations.

Minimum expectations establish boundaries. Most people want to stay in bounds.

To make a minimum expectation reasonable, always provide some explanation of *why*. The phrase "at least" indicates the minimum need. For example:
- "Having at least two days notice before a meeting gives me adequate time to prepare and schedule. This also ensures better use of my time and yours and a more effective meeting."
- "It would help me if you could get this information to me by at least 9:00 a.m. each Tuesday. This enables me to complete my work by noon, which is the deadline set by our customers."

Improvement

Improvement is:
1. making better or becoming better,
2. an increase in value,
3. a better condition.

Improvement

Security and stability require continuous improvement.

Predictability is becoming increasingly difficult:
- We do not know from day to day the price of energy or money.
- We do not know who our competitors will be or where they will come from.
- Worst of all, sometimes we do not even know who our customers are.

In the future, not changing will *increase* insecurity and instability. We ignore improvement opportunities by overlooking new ways of doing things.

Our future security and stability depends on how quickly, how efficiently, and how effectively we continuously improve.

Improvement always requires change

Improvement

Improvement always requires change.

Experience teaches everything about a job, except how to improve it.
"If experience taught us something, why are we in such a mess?" -
W. Edwards Deming

Things that do not change remain the same...or get worse. Trying
harder at the same thing gives you more of the same thing. If you lose
25 cents on each hamburger you sell, selling twice as many is not a
good idea.

Insanity is doing the same old thing, the same old way...and expecting
a different result. "It's very simple. Dull yesterday—dull today—dull
tomorrow." - Tom Peters

"You can never do it better until you are allowed to do it differently." -
Earl Fray

Improvement

Change never guarantees improvement.

A change is not successful unless it adds value by resulting in improvement.

Just because something is different does not mean it is better. Change can sometimes make things worse.

If employees feel punished by management because a change they implemented did not achieve improvement, employees' innovation and creativity for future improvement will wither.

If a change does not result in improvement, going back to normal ensures no improvement. Improvement requires a different change.

Improvement

Reorganizing, by itself, improves nothing.

Changing the organizational structure does not necessarily change the way individuals do their work.

Quality and service will not improve unless processes (the way people do their work) change.

Reorganizing can make it easier—or more difficult—for people to change the way they do their work.

Management may be the worst judge of the effectiveness and value of a reorganization.

Strategies are approved in executive committees that common sense dictates are bound to fail. The problem is—common sense is not commonly practiced.

Improvement

Getting in the groove can become a rut.

One foggy night, a man decided to take the shortcut home through the cemetery. Having difficulty seeing, he was feeling his way between the headstones when he fell into an open grave. Realizing where he was, he first tried to jump out. That did not work. He tried to climb out. That did not work. In fact, nothing worked. Exhausted, he sunk into the corner and said to himself, "I'll have to wait until morning and yell for help. There's nothing I can do now."

So, he squatted down into a corner and went to sleep...until he was awakened by a noise! Someone else just fell into the same hole.

The second man did not notice the first man already there.

Improvement

—continued from previous page

Trying to get out, the second man jumped, but did not make it. He jumped again. Meanwhile, the first man was very entertained watching the second guy try to get out.

Eventually, the second man became exhausted. While leaning against the side of the grave catching his breath, the second man was startled to hear a voice from the darkness exclaim,
"YOU'LL NEVER GET OUT OF HERE!...."

But he did...Fright powered him out of the hole!

Moral of the story: Sometimes it takes a fresh point of view, a new perspective to get out of a groove that, if you are not careful, could become your grave! Do not bury yourself by always doing more of the same thing. *Improvement requires change.*

Improvement

"We have met the enemy...It is us."

- Pogo, by Walt Kelly

In a bureaucratic system, many are discouraged from implementing change because they assume that all improvement must come from changing policies or regulations. All power seems to be in the hands of the mythical *they*. "Until *they* make changes, there's nothing I can do...."

We give "them" power over us, letting "them" or "it" do our thinking for us. "This is the way we do things here." "We've always done it this way."

However, even in a bureaucracy, or maybe especially in a bureaucracy, we are "they." Since you, individually, cannot change everything, focus on implementing changes within your sphere of influence.

Improvement

All improvement lies in the process.

Improvement comes from changing the process or changing how tasks are performed.

Changing how tasks are performed requires changing one of the following:
- *methods*: the way an individual performs a task;
- *procedures*: the formal, prescribed way an organization wants a task performed;
- *tools*: software, hardware, check lists, etc. a person uses to perform a task;
- *equipment*: hardware (a capital expenditure), used to perform a task;
- *skill level* of the person performing a task.

Improvement

Treat attitude as an *effect*, the result of experience, instead of the cause of people's behavior.

People's attitudes stem from what they experience. For example:
- If some children are afraid of swimming, they always will be until they have a good experience swimming.
- If some children hate school, they always will until they have a good experience in school.
- If some people hate work, they always will until what they experience at work improves.

For people's attitude to improve, they must first have or foresee a better *experience*.

Improvement

Focus improvement on the process, not on people's attitudes.

Threatening, bribing, or cajoling will get action. You may even coerce someone into doing exactly as you desire. This improvement will not last, because it is only movement. It will only be momentary movement because all the burden is on you, the mover, to make sure others do the moving.

Changing the way something is done (the process), whether it is swimming, learning, or working, can achieve improvement. "We focus on the process because it is within our sphere of influence—attitudes are not." - Ernie Wessman

Improving what is done also virtually always improves attitude.

In business, if you stay the same, you will fall behind.

Improvement

In business, if you stay the same, you will fall behind.

In the past, people tied security and stability to *no* changes:
- "It's been good enough in the past. Why change?"
- "It's not broken. Why are you trying to fix it?"
- "We've always done it this way."
- "This is the way we do things here."

Your competitors do not stay the same. The world does not stay the same. Staying the same guarantees no improvement.

If the going gets easy, you may be going downhill.

If you do not *continuously* improve, you will fall behind.

Improvement

To focus improvement efforts on the process, assume everyone is trying hard and doing their best.

Urging, coaxing, intimidating or threatening someone to try harder does not increase the person's ability to improve.

Assuming people are doing their best does *not* also mean assuming their best is good enough. Good intentions do not insure good work.

If your best is not good enough, you must change your process, the way you do things.

When the process improves, usually attitudes also improve.

Improvement

"Do or do not. There is no try."

- Yoda, Jedi Knight Master

There is a scene in the second Star Wars movie, "The Empire Strikes Back," which illustrates what many people go through when trying to achieve improvement.

Luke Skywalker has gone to the distant planet Degaba searching for Yoda, the Jedi Knight Master, and crash-lands in a swamp. He meets Yoda who later tries to teach young Skywalker about the ways of a Jedi knight. At one point in his training, Luke tries to use the force to raise his fighter out of the swamp, but fails. Luke complains to Yoda, "We'll never get it out now."

Yoda replies, "So certain are you. Always with you it can't be done. Do you hear nothing that I say?"
☞

Improvement

—continued from previous page

Luke then responds, "Master, moving stones around is one thing, but this is *totally* different."

"No, no different!" says Yoda. "Only different in your *mind*. You must *unlearn* what you have learned." Luke sighs and says, "All right, I'll give it a try."

Yoda snaps right back, "NO, Try not. **DO or do not.** There is no *try*!"

Luke then tries again to use the power of the force to raise his fighter from the swamp. But after raising it a little, it slowly sinks deeper into the mire. Luke responds in discouragement, "I can't...It's too big..."

People often respond to the need for improvement by saying
☛

Improvement

—continued from previous page

that it's too big. Why try? After all, we've always done it this way....

Yoda says to Luke, "Size matters not." Then he tries to teach Luke about the power of the force. Luke listens begrudgingly and then, giving up, says, "You want the *impossible*."

Yoda then uses the power of the force to raise the fighter from the swamp and move it to dry land. Luke is astonished. He exclaims, "I don't...I don't believe it!"

Yoda concludes, "*That* is why you fail."

Moral of the story: Trying harder to do more of the same thing, the same way, produces more of the same thing. Luke Skywalker had to change the way he was using the force. No change guarantees no improvement.

Improvement

"There is no *instant* pudding!"

- W. Edwards Deming

Each time improvement is wanted, it would be so much easier if there were just one wonderful, painless, all-encompassing change that would guarantee improvement. A *quick* fix would also be very desirable.

There is almost never such a change to be found.

Programs, banners, posters, buzz words, and slogans do not achieve improvement. Big improvement requires continuous, incremental changes in the work process. Long term commitment is required.

Continuous improvement must be viewed as a journey, not a destination.

Improvement

Change always costs.

Making a change costs time, effort, and sometimes money.

Change always increases uncertainty. The cost of change varies significantly depending on whether people *perceive* the changes as:
- non-disruptive,
- manageable disruption, or
- unmanageable disruption.

Implementing change almost always involves some kind of learning-curve, meaning time to learn the new ways.

Effectively managing change, although not eliminating the cost of change, minimizes it.

Improvement

Improvement always pays.

Sustaining or increasing quality and service requires continuously adding value to work processes, products, and services. In today's world, there is no such thing as staying the same. Whenever we stagnate individually or organizationally, degradation sets in.

If you are not continuously improving, you will be overrun by competitors who are. Continuous improvement is basic to future security and stability.

Improvement always pays because it adds value.

Effectively managing change maximizes value added by an improvement.

Managing Change

Effectively managing change minimizes cost while maximizing improvement.

When will things get back to the good-old-days?... Never.

Managing Change

When will things get back to the good-old-days?...Never!

Wherever we live, it has been hotter than usual, colder than usual, wetter than usual, dryer than usual. We yearn for the good-old-days, wanting things to get back to normal.

They never will. First of all, the old-days were not that good, and second of all, which normal year do you want to get back to!?

Today, loving change, tumult, even chaos is a prerequisite for survival—let alone success.

To meet the demands of the fast changing, competitive scene, we must learn to love change as much as we hated it in the past.

Managing Change

The goal of changing should be achieving improvement.

Change for the sake of changing only costs time, effort, and sometimes money.

Without change, there can never be improvement.

Establishing the goal of continuous improvement means you will never arrive at the point where no more improvement is required.

Continuous improvement requires continuously changing.

The two goals of managing change are:
- minimizing the cost of change,
- maximizing improvement from change.

Managing Change

"We ourselves must be the change we wish to see in others." - Mahatma Gandhi

An aircraft carrier pulls out of the harbor on a foggy night. A sailor up on deck sees they are headed right for a light through the fog. He flashes a signal: "We are on a collision course. Change course."

A signal flashes back: "You're right. We are on a collision course. You change course."

The sailor tries another signal: "This is the aircraft carrier. We are on a collision course. Change course!"

A signal returns: "I already told you, I know we are on a collision course. You change course!"

☞

Managing Change

—continued from previous page

The sailor decides he needs more authority. He awakens the admiral and explains the situation. The admiral commands: "Send this message: 'This is the *Admiral of the fleet*. Change course!!'"

The response flashes back: "This is the keeper of lighthouse! *You* change course!!"

Moral of the story: it is always easy to see the need for change in everyone except yourself. You have total control over changing you!

Managing Change

Managing change by *compliance* is easy to initiate, but difficult to manage.

Managing change by forcing or demanding compliance places the burden on management to ensure that employees comply with changes implemented:
- *Focus* is on the employee.
- *Responsibility* for making the change successful is on the manager responsible for implementing the change.
- *Communication direction* is AT the employee.
- *Management climate* is dictorial.

Forcing compliance does little to guarantee actual improvement, because with compliance, the goal is implement a change instead of achieve improvement.

Managing Change

Managing change by *commitment* is difficult to initiate, but easy to manage.

Managing change by voluntary commitment requires those changing to assume the obligation for improvement:

- *Focus* is on improvement to be achieved from changes implemented.
- *Responsibility* for making the change successful is on those actually putting the change to use.
- *Communication direction* is WITH the employee.
- *Management climate* is collaborative.

Obtaining commitment virtually ensures improvement, because the goal is not implementing a change, but attaining improvement.

If no improvement results from a change, it simply means a different change is required.

Managing Change

Start small, where you are most likely to succeed.

Minimize the cost of change by starting small:
- Small does not mean trivial or insignificant.
- Starting small means, do an experiment.
- Limit the scope of what is changed. Do not try to change everyone or everything all at once.
- Limit the duration of the experiment. Evaluate the change within a specific time frame.

Maximize improvement from change by starting where you are most likely to succeed:
- Small, quick successes build credibility, trust and momentum.
- Additional modifications that may be required to insure full improvement are easier to identify.
- People learn faster from success than failure.

Managing Change

People resist even the most trivial change.

Many people seem perfectly willing to endure a bad situation that is known rather than to face any uncertainty a change may bring.

Individuals will resist change until they are comfortable with the following:
- What will the change do *to* me?
- What will the change do *for* me?
- How will the change affect my relationships with others?

Even with this information, some reluctance is understandable. Eliminating uncertainty requires actually experiencing the change.

Managing Change

Minimize uncertainty in the transition period.

Uncertainty significantly increases the cost of any change. Uncertainty encourages apprehension, misgivings, and skepticism about change instead of commitment to improvement.

Uncertainty arises from insufficient communication. No news is always assumed to mean bad news. Lack of communication spawns rumors which attack morale and drain productivity.

To eliminate uncertainty, information must be frequent, absolutely honest, and from credible sources. This means sometimes the answer to a question will be "That has not been decided yet" or "I don't know, but I will find out and let you know."

To improve, use what you learn.

Managing Change

To improve, use what you learn.

An old Chinese story: There once was a group of turkeys that wanted to learn how to fly. So, they appointed one among them to be the turkey trainer and set aside a day for the training. Great preparation was made for a day of training and celebration. Finally, the long anticipated day arrived, and the training was fantastic. They studied takeoffs. They studied landings. They pondered the glory of soaring through the clouds and gliding into the sunset. When the day was over and the training completed, everyone agreed that the training had been out standing... and they all *walked* home together....

- as told by Merlin R. Lybbert

Moral of the story: You must use what you learn. Do not be a turkey. Improvement requires implementing change.

Effective Leadership

Leadership is the ability to influence others.

***Effective* Leadership is the ability to influence others to continuously improve.**

Effective Leadership

Effective leaders make the right things happen.

There are three types of people in organizations:
1) those who make things happen - these are the leaders;
2)those who watch what happens;
3) those who wonder, "What happened?"

Negative leaders are trouble makers, making the wrong things happen, influencing others to cause problems and prevent progress.

Effective leaders make the right things happen, influencing others to continuously improve.

"Acid test for excellence: would you want your son or daughter to work here?" - Tom Peters

Effective Leadership

Traditional Management   VS.   Effective Leadership

- *React* to problems.
- *Fix* problems.
- *Blame* the guilty so they will be properly motivated not to do it again.
- Use *authority*: tell people what to do and how to do it.
- Act like a *COP*; review, evaluate, and inspect to make sure people are doing what they were told to do.
- *"I'll* do all the thinking."
- Emphasize *compliance* with policies, rules, and regulations.

- *Anticipate* problems.
- *Prevent* problems by changing the process.
- Identify what in the *process* is causing problems.
- Use *influence*: focus on customers' needs, ask the right questions.
- Be a *COACH*; enable people to continuously improve, identify what must change.
- "What do *you* think?"
- Get *commitment* to continuous improvement of all work processes.

Effective Leadership

Authority does not insure effective leadership.

A little authority can lead to a lot of misuse. The "My way or the high way!" misuse of authority influences people to hide problems, to have someone ready to blame, and to do only what they are told—regardless of the consequences to customers or co-workers.

The "I'll do all the thinking!" misuse of authority discourages innovation, creativity and new ideas, and thus prevents continuous improvement.

Use authority to establish constancy of purpose for the organization's mission. Use authority to lead people into continuous improvement. Use authority to provide resources necessary to maintain quality and service as well as enable continuous improvement.

Effective Leadership

The most valuable skill on earth is the ability to influence others to continuously improve.

The most valuable skill for parents is the ability to influence their children to continuously improve.

The most valuable skill for teachers is the ability to influence their students to continuously improve.

Since people are the most valuable resource any organization has, the most valuable skill for managers and supervisors is the ability to influence their subordinates to continuously improve.

Skills for influencing must be established on a foundation of trust. Techniques will not compensate for a lack of trust.

Effective Leadership

Effective leaders *enable* continuous improvement.

Leaders are *enablers* when they:

- authorize,
- allow,
- permit,
- sanction,
- prepare,
- condition,
- qualify,
- influence,

- empower,
- give strength,
- give competence,
- render able,
- capacitate,
- facilitate,
- encourage,
- reinforce.

What if the effectiveness of leaders were evaluated by how much continuous improvement they enabled? One way to quantify how much enabling takes place is to ask how much time employees are allowed *each* week, aside from daily work, to focus on improving their work process.

Effective Leadership

Using authority influences, but not always for *continuous* improvement.

Authority used to catch people doing something wrong will find wrong things increasing. What you expect is what you get.

Authority used to blame and punish the guilty will find that creativity and innovation shut down.

Authority used to reinforce people doing something right, will find right things increasing.

Authority used to supply whatever enables improvement will find improvement increasing.

Effective Leadership

Malicious compliance results in every-one losing.

Malicious compliance is doing what you are told *knowing* that it is wrong.

Malicious compliance occurs when people must do whatever they are told, no questions asked. Malicious compliance can be forced by the boss or a customer.

Malicious compliance results in unnecessary repair of equipment, unnecessary replacement of items, and unnecessary work being done.

From the workers' perspective, malicious compliance is never their fault. They are just doing what they have been told—as commanded. Customers, management, and workers all lose in malicious compliance.

Effective Leadership

Empowering does not ensure productive thinking.

Empowering employees is good if they know how to channel their thinking into delighting customers and improving quality. It is not enough to give people permission to think for themselves and then expect continuous improvement to endlessly flow forth.

Controlling quality and service requires a system of methods, procedures, tools, equipment, and skill level. Establishing a way to measure quality and service also enables evaluation of process changes.

With a system of control and a means of measurement in place, employees can think for themselves, innovate to meet customers' needs and change processes to continuously improve quality.

Knowing the right question is more important than knowing the right answers.

Effective Leadership

Knowing the right question is more important than knowing the right answers.

Many people have never learned to think for themselves. They never had to. There was always the right answer in the back of the book, or someone they could go to for the right answer.

Always providing the right answer stifles learning.

The right question influences others to think for themselves.

Discovering the answer for themselves (resulting from the right question) results in ownership of the solution as well as ownership of the problem.

Effective Leadership

Commitment to change requires tolerating failure.

"Nothing great or grand was ever achieved while trying to avoid failure."   - Earl Fray

Tolerating failure is not giving in to failure. Tolerating failure means taking a long-term view to continuous improvement, instead of always looking for the quick fix.

Since improvement requires change, but change never guarantees improvement, implementing changes could make things worse.

Punishing poor short-term results from changes shuts down thinking and nurtures malicious compliance. No one will risk making a change if poor results or even failure are not tolerated.

Effective Leadership

Clearly define your target before trying to hit it.

One day in the old West, a cowboy stepped off the train and the first thing he noticed was a bullseye painted on the side of a fence at the train station. He paid no attention because, after all, in the old West people did a lot of target practice.

However, when he walked to the middle of town, he saw thousands of bullseyes, on the sides of barns, on buildings, on fences, on the board walk. He also noticed there was only *one* bullet hole, dead-center in each target.

"This is mighty curious," he thought. So, he began asking who was doing all the target practice. His search finally led him to the town idiot.

101

Effective Leadership

—continued from previous page

Anxious to satisfy his curiosity, the cowboy asked the idiot,
"How do you hit the bullseye dead-center each time!?"

"It's easy," the idiot responded. "You shoot first and draw the bullseye
after!"

Moral of the story: Too often we strive for goals like the idiot in this
story. Sometimes we expend great effort without first clearly defining
the goal. Know exactly what your target is before you fire any shots.

Sometimes performance appraisal seems to also use a variation of the
idiot's approach: after the work is all done, hold people accountable for
goals that were not achievable. Since this is obviously unfair, all you
can do is appraise how hard they tried (how many shots were fired)
and how busy they appeared (how they looked while firing).

Effective Leadership

Goals + pain or gain = deceitful accounting.

Threats and intimidation, or rewards and bonuses for making the numbers look good leads to creative accounting with the intent to deceive.

Deceitful accounting means lying.

Poor quality work is tolerated or excused when quantity or quotas are the only goal. Teamwork is given only lip service when you are only accountable for how much *you* get done.

It does not matter how good the numbers look, if customers are not delighted. You cannot fake quality or service with customers.

Effective Leadership

Effectiveness has higher priority than Efficiency.

Efficiency is doing the job right.
Effectiveness is doing the right job.

Efficiency focuses on cost.
Effectiveness focuses on value.

Doing trivial things very efficiently has little value. Nobody cares how efficient you are, if you are not effective.

Once you are doing the right job, improving your efficiency increases the value of your effectiveness.

Effective Leadership

Make sure everyone pulls in the same direction.

Small differences in understanding about priorities can cause large differences in results. Two questions help ensure everyone pulls in the same direction:

1) "Who is your most important customer?" This question clarifies whose needs are most important.

2) "What is the most important work you do?" This question identifies each person's perception of the most important use of time.

If boss and subordinates, or if co-workers among themselves do not agree with the answers to these two questions, everyone will pull in different directions. This attacks quality, service, and morale.

Effective Leadership

Meetings should focus more on effectiveness than efficiency.

Efficient meetings streamline the use of meeting time.
Effective meetings accomplish desired results.

To ensure *each* meeting is effective, ask, "When we leave *this* meeting, what will have been *accomplished*?" For each agenda item, determine the desired results:

Agenda Item
- discuss issues
- look into problems
- go over the latest information
- coordinate efforts

Desired Results
- priorities clarified
- three alternatives identified
- impact on current priorities identified.
- resources shifted to current priority

Effective Leadership

People respond to what they are held accountable for.

Responsibility is the obligation to perform work.
ACCOUNTABILITY is the obligation to get desired results.

Performing duties and working hard do not necessarily insure desired results.

Establishing accountability requires feedback on quality and service, meaning: feedback on what is accomplished and how is it delivered.

Accountability should come from the customer's perspective: "Do we delight internal and external customers with our quality and service?"

Effective Leadership

To be accountable, people must have control.

Lousy Leadership: "Follow me—but not so close." Restraining, repressing, holding back, or keeping down facilitates no improvement.

When you only expect people to do what they are told, they are not accountable for quality or service. Whoever tells them what to do is accountable.

When you expect people to think for themselves and make their own decisions—they will.

People who *feel* accountable for their quality and service take pride in what they do.

Customer Service

Customer service means *delighting* all the customers.

Customer service concentrates on how quality is delivered.

The only purpose for any job is to delight all the customers.

Customer Service

The only purpose for any job is to delight all the customers.

You satisfy customers if you meet their expectations. To delight customers, you must *exceed* expectations.

A customer is anyone who receives or uses your output.

Internal customers are those within your organization who receive or use your output. External customers are those external to your organization.

First meeting *internal* customers' needs creates the capacity to delight external customers.

Customer Service

Meaningful feedback from customers enables improvement.

Complaints do not necessarily *enable* improvement. Fixing a current problem will not automatically prevent the problem from recurring.

Knowing something is wrong does not necessarily identify where change is needed. To enable improvement, feedback from customers must identify what needs to change.

Instead of using feedback to simply react to current problems, feedback should also be used to *anticipate* customers' future needs.

Anticipating customers' future needs is essential to continuous improvement.

Customer Service

Your best is not good enough until all customers are delighted.

Mothers teach their children to do their best. Teachers encourage their students to do their best. However, on the job, you are not paid to do your best. You are paid to delight all the customers.

If simply doing your best is the goal, you can view yourself as your own customer, which means the only one you have to worry about delighting is yourself.

If your best is not good enough to delight customers, to improve, you must change the way you do your work.

Customer Service

Your enemy may be your customer.

"You can never please *them*. They are *never* satisfied."
"If it were not for *you*, my job would be a lot easier around here!"
"If they call, tell them I'm not here!"

Sometimes the people who seem to give us the hardest time are in reality our customers, those who receive our output— and are not delighted.

Customers' needs *continually* upgrade, which means they always want more, better, faster, and cheaper.

You do not have to love customers, not even like them. Just delight them! To delight them, you must provide world class quality and service, and *continuously* improve.

Customer Service

Keeping your eye on the goal prevents falling into activity traps.

One afternoon, a grandfather and his grandson were walking home across the snow covered field toward the farm house. The young grandson decided to challenge his grandfather.

"Grandpa, let's have a contest to see who can walk the straightest line across the field."

The grandpa agreed and off they started. While the grandpa strode easily through the snow, the grandson was very careful making sure that each step was exactly in front of the previous step.
☞

Customer Service

—continued from previous page

When the grandson finally arrived at the farm house, he turned to inspect his trail and found his line was not nearly as straight as grandpa's.

"Why is your line so much straighter than mine?" asked the grandson.

"Well, you see this tree, right here in front of us," responded grandpa. "I just kept my eye on it and headed right toward it!"

Moral of the story: Goals give you direction. Do not get caught in activity traps where being busy and trying hard becomes more important than achieving the goal.

Customer Service

To delight customers, you must fully understand their needs.

Customers are not delighted unless their needs are met. To meet their needs, you must first understand them.

To fully understand customers' needs, ask the *5Ws1H*:
- *who* needs it,
- *what* is needed,
- *where* is it needed,
- *when* is it needed.
- *why* is it needed,
- *how* will it be used

Knowing *why* customers want something and *how* they will use it, often describes customers' needs better than what they say they want.

Being busy is not the same as getting results.

Customer Service

Being busy is not the same as getting results.

After examinations had been graded and returned, some of the college students wanted to negotiate for partial credit. They reasoned that although they did not get the right answer or did not finish some of the questions, they came close—they were on the right track—they had the right approach.

Granting partial credit in the class room is appropriate and often helpful. However, in the real world it does not matter how hard you tried or how busy you were or how much time you put in—if you did not achieve desired results.

Being busy does not necessarily mean meeting customers' needs.

Customer Service

Avoid this assumption: "It's clear to me, therefore, it's clear to you."

Those serving customers can easily make the assumption that since they know exactly what they mean, so do the customers.

Sometimes we hear a version of this assumption at home:
"I know that's what I said, but that's not what I meant—."
"Why didn't you say what you meant?"
"I did, but you were not listening—. In fact, you never listen—. In fact, you've got a bad attitude!"

Avoid this assumption by understanding the other's point of view and speak to *their* understanding.

Customer Service

The customer is *not* always right.

Sometimes what customers want is not what they actually *need*. If this is the case, you will not delight them when you give them what they want, until they have what they really need. This is also true in raising children.

Customers rarely recognize when what they want is not actually what they need.

Asking customers the *5Ws1H* (who, what, where, when, why, and how) helps clarify their needs for them and you.

Customer Service

Whenever the boss is the primary customer, thinking shuts down.

In traditional management, the boss is the primary customer. Some supervisors instruct subordinates, "Your job is to make *me* happy. Your job is to make *me* look good."

If people sense that their only job is to please the boss, they will only do what the boss says—even if this displeases customers. To do otherwise might displease the boss. This causes thinking to shut down.

You can recognize shut-down thinking when you hear:
- "Don't ask me. I just work here."
- "That's not my job."
- "I'm just doing what I have been told."
- "Let me transfer your call to someone who cares."

Customer Service

Pay particular attention to *un*realistic customer demands.

Ignoring customer demands because they are unrealistic stifles continuous improvement.

Unrealistic demands are those that you currently cannot achieve and never will achieve if you continue to do business the same way.

If your competitors *anticipated* your customers' demands, they already implemented changes that will now meet your customers' needs— leaving you behind.

Sensitivity to future, unrealistic demands helps you anticipate changes you need to implement today.

Quality

Quality consists of the value delivered to customers.

Join the Quality Revolution
or be overrun by it.

Quality

Join the Quality Revolution or be overrun by it.

THE QUALITY REVOLUTION

1. **Meet the standard:** means a product or service meets some standard or set of specifications.

2. **Meet customers' needs:** means a product or service delights the user *and* meets standards.

3. **Meet costs:** means improve quality while driving costs DOWN *and* meet customers needs *and* meet standards. To drive costs down while maintaining or improving quality requires reducing variation in work processes.

4. **Anticipate customers' needs:** means meet customers' needs before customers are aware of those needs (for example, development of the Sony Walkman) *and* meet standards *and* current customers' needs *and* meet costs.

Each phase adds to the previous in difficulty and value.

Quality

Simple definition: Quality is whatever it takes to delight all the customers.

World class quality is what delights customers. *World class* means you are as good or better than anyone, anywhere at what you do.

Ben & Jerry's Ice Cream delights their customers across the country. The formal test that a new ice cream flavor has to pass at Ben & Jerry's: "Is it weird enough?"

Sometimes what delights one customer, causes problems for another customer. The issue then becomes: who is the most important customer?

If the boss is pleased, but the customers are unhappy, the boss is insensitive to who the real customers are.

Quality

More sophisticated definition: Quality means minimizing variation in quality characteristics.

For example:
- Minimize variation in *accuracy* - eliminate errors.
- Minimize variation in *timeliness* - always meet the dealine.
- Minimize variation in *thoroughness* - never leave anything out.
- Minimize variation in *safety* - no lost time due to accidents.
- Minimize variation in *understandability* - no misunderstandings.

Minimizing variation in quality characteristics is a never-ending journey.

Quality

Dangerously wrong and woefully inadequate definition: Quality means meeting specifications.

The goal is not to meet specifications. The goal is to delight customers with world class quality.

Meeting specifications or some standard is the *minimum* expectation. You should *at least* meet specifications, but this will not necessarily delight customers.

Similarly, finishing a job does not guarantee world class quality. Complying with rules, regulations, policies, and procedures does not ensure world class service. Doing what you are told does not mean that customers are delighted.

Quality

The quality of work determines the quality of output.

Quality of the process used to perform work determines quality of the work.

Continuous improvement of work quality requires continuous improvement of the following five parts of a work process:
- *methods* - the way an individual performs a task;
- *procedures* - the formal, prescribed way an organization wants a task performed;
- *tools* - software, hardware and check lists a person uses to perform a task;
- *equipment* - hardware (a capital expenditure) used to perform a task;
- *skill level* of the person performing a task.

Quality

You will never be better than what is supplied.

Output will never be better than the input received from suppliers.
For example:
- if input has errors, output is inaccurate;
- if input is late, output is not timely;
- if input has omissions, output is incomplete;
- if input is misunderstood, output is unreliable.

Input from internal and external suppliers consists of resources
required to perform work, including:
- information
- materials
- personnel
- facilities
- budget
- equipment
- schedules.

Quality

The quality of suppliers' work determines the quality of input.

To produce world class quality and service, suppliers must provide world class input for workers. Suppliers can be internal or external to your organization.

To enable suppliers to provide world class input:
1. ensure suppliers understand *who* needs it, *what* you need, *where* you need it, *when* you need it, *why* you need it, and *how* you will use what is supplied;
2. provide suppliers with timely, meaningful feedback helping them to:
   - evaluate how well they meet your needs, *and*
   - anticipate your future needs.

Quality

Total Quality involves everyone in continuous improvement.

Continuous improvement of quality is a team-fueled, customer-focused approach to doing business. The team consists of suppliers, workers, and customers. Management should be suppliers and coaches for workers.

Continuous improvement of output requires:
- continuous improvement of the work process *and*
- continuous improvement of input *and*
- continuous improvement of suppliers' work processes.

Total Quality will not happen unless there is a foundation of trust. You cannot fake trust anymore than you can fake quality.

Controlling Quality and Service

No feedback means out of control.

Control of operations, equipment, or systems is a function of feedback. No feedback means there is no way to gauge or evaluate whatever you want to control. Quality and service, not people, need to be controlled.

Accurate control requires accurate feedback.

Timely control requires timely feedback.

Tight control requires frequent feedback.

A difficult part of controlling quality and service is deciding what specific feedback will ensure adequate control of quality and service.

Controlling Quality
and Service

**Control is key to maintaining *and*
continuously improving
quality and service.**

Controlling Quality and Service

No complaints means nothing.

No complaints may be good, if customers are delighted but are just not telling you. However, this is not likely.

No complaints often means people feel that complaining would not make any difference anyway. Therefore, they give up trying to get improvement from you.

No complaints is devastating if customers are totally displeased and do not tell you that they went somewhere else—and tell all their friends to do the same.

No complaints means no feedback, which means no way to evaluate or control quality and service.

After-the-fact measurements do not control quality.

Controlling Quality and Service

After-the-fact measurements do not control quality.

After-the-fact measurements of quality focus on the finished output.

Measuring the quality of output does not control the quality of work while doing the work. For example:
- Counting the number of errors in a letter does not improve letter writing.
- Statistics on failed landings do not help the pilot make a good landing.

Such measurements identify but do not control the quality of output. The quality of work controls quality of output.

Controlling Quality and Service

Authority does not control quality or service.

The fact that parents have legal authority over their children does not give them the ability to control their behavior.

Authority over others does not control the quality of the work they perform. The *process* used in doing the work controls quality and service.

Authority is the right to make decisions. Using authority to order, direct, or command quality work puts all of the burden on the one with authority to ensure quality and service. In reality, the people doing the work determine the quality and service. Therefore, they should feel responsible and be accountable.

Controlling Quality and Service

Inspection of output does not ensure future quality.

Bureaucratic managers and supervisors spend hours inspecting memos and reports to *make sure* that they are complete, understandable, and accurate. Often the writing is red-lined and sent back for rewriting until the subordinate adequately guesses the way the boss really wants it to read—an incredible waste of time.

Instead of encouraging improvement, constant rewriting by the boss causes the subordinate to say, "Why don't you just write it yourself!"

Inspection, rework, and reprocessing, are not corrective action on the *work process*. Improving the result *this time*, does not guarantee any better future results, unless the process improves.

Just because the numbers look good, does not mean quality and service are in control.

Controlling Quality and Service

Just because your numbers look good, does not mean quality and service are in control.

Suppose a surgeon wanted to control the quantity, quality, and efficiency of his operations. He might track the number of stitches per inch applied per operation, the time required for each operation, and the promptness of surgical team members.

Based on these measurable indicators, he might claim with pride that according to all the numbers, his operations were very successful...even though all the patients died.

Do not get lost among the numbers. Make sure indicators measure what most needs controlling.

143

Controlling Quality and Service

The drive-in-window approach gives no lasting improvement.

People tend to overreact, looking for a quick fix to a problem that really requires a *system* change: "We don't have time for a permanent fix right now. Do whatever you have to to meet this deadline."

This drive-in window, quick-fix approach to problem solving is why so many organizations are in deep trouble today.

Quality experts agree[*] that 85% of problems are recurring problems that employees describe as typical, usual, or normal. These type of problems require changing the work process, which means changing methods, procedures, tools, equipment, or skill level.

[*] *The Deming Route to Quality and Productivity*, W.W. Scherkenbach, Quality Press, 1988, p. 101.

Controlling Quality and Service

To maintain quality and service, control the work process.

The quality of most work is out of control because no system exists to control the work process *in progress*.

How the work is done determines the quality of the work. A work system consisting of the following determines how work is done:
- *methods* - the way an individual performs a task;
- *procedures* - the formal, prescribed way an organization wants a task performed;
- *tools* - software, hardware, and check lists a person uses to perform a task;
- *equipment* - hardware (a capital expenditure) used to perform a task;
- *skill level* of the person performing a task.

Controlling Quality and Service

If you cannot define it, you cannot control it.

If you do not know where you are going, any road will take you there. If you aim at nothing, you hit it!

Can you define what *you* mean by the following:
- speak *clearly*,
- work *safely*,
- finish *quickly*,
- write *understandably*,
- answer *courteously*,
- analyze *thoroughly*.

If you cannot define the above characteristics of quality and service in terms that are *observable*, you have no way to know if, when, or how well you achieve them.

Controlling Quality and Service

To focus control, define quality in terms of quality characteristics.

To focus quality control, define performance of work in terms of quality characteristics such as the following:

Accuracy	Friendliness	Efficiency
Thoroughness	Courtesy	Effectiveness
Timeliness	Understandability	Reliability
Consistency	Clarity	Repeatability
Safety	Conciseness	Dependability
Legality	Completeness	Adequacy
Relevancy	Neatness	Cleanliness

Controlling Quality and Service

Controlling one quality characteristic does not ensure control of the others.

Timely does not mean thorough.

Accurate does not mean understandable.

Complete does not mean concise.

Efficient does not mean effective.

Friendly does not mean dependable.

Quick does not mean safe.

Legal does not mean honest.

Controlling Quality and Service

Each quality characteristic requires its own work system.

Having methods to ensure timeliness does not ensure safety. In fact, methods used to do a job quickly might conflict with doing the job safely. Procedures to ensure work is done legally do not ensure that work is done efficiently.

To control characteristics such as timeliness and efficiency, a work system must be designed for each quality characteristic you want to control. A work system consists of methods, procedures, tools, equipment, and skill level.

Without a work system matched to quality characteristics, people can only do their best, which means quality is out of control.

Controlling Quality and Service

Sufficiently controlling the quality of work guarantees quality of output.

Suppose you want to guarantee timeliness of output. You would need a work system designed for doing the job in a timely fashion. This work system would consist of:
- *methods* for doing the job in a timely fashion,
- *procedures* written to ensure timeliness of the tasks per formed,
- *tools* to facilitate timeliness of the work,
- *equipment* designed and employed to ensure timeliness of the work,
- *skills* enabling timeliness of the work.

Using this work system would control timeliness of the work and therefore guarantee timeliness of the output.

Controlling Quality and Service

The five Evils measure process performance.

The 5 Evils are *defects, mistakes, delay, waste, and accident/injury*. Each of the 5 Evils has a direct impact on the cost of operations and customer satisfaction. If a problem demonstrates no impact in terms of defects, mistakes, delay, waste, accident/injury, it is not a problem.

Each of the five Evils is *verifiable* in terms of the following:
- *Who* is having the problem (Is the problem with one person or a particular department or shift?)
- *What* is the problem (How many of the 5 Evils are due to the same problem?)
- *Where* is the problem occurring (Is one peice of equipment causing the problem or is it in the system?)
- When is the problem occurring (Is there a trend or pattern to any of the 5 Evils?)

Understanding the above will help determine why there is a problem which enables solutions that prevent future problems.

Notes on Sources

page 2   Elbert Hubbard (1856-1915), American lecturer, publisher, editor, and essayist.

page 5   "quiet lives of desperation," a phrase used by Henry David Thoreau (1817-1862), author of *Walden*.

page 17   Truman Madsen, Professor of philosophy and religion, Brigham Young University, adapted from *Eternal Man*, Deseret Book, 1966, p. 57.

page 21   Stephen R. Covey, chairman of the Covey Leadership Center, *The 7 Habits of Highly Effective People*, Fireside, 1989, p. 235.

page 22   Joseph Juran, Chairman emeritus, Juran Institute, elder statesman of total quality control in America; see *Quality Control Handbook*, McGraw-Hill, third edition, pp. 2-16 to 2-19 for further discussion.

page 57   W. Edwards Deming (1900-1993), consultant, Distinguished Professor in Management, Columbia U., senior guru of statistical quality control, Japan's Deming Prize named in his honor.

page 57   Tom Peters, lecturer, co-author of *In Search of Excellence*, author of *Thriving on Chaos* and *Liberation Management*.

page 57	Earl Fray, General Manager, EG&G.
page 65	Ernie Wessman, Vice President, PacifiCorp.
page 72	W. Edwards Deming, see page 57.
page 79	Mahatma Gandhi (1869-1948), helped free India from British control, honored by the people of India as the father of their nation.
page 87	Merlin R. Lybbert, attorney, General Authority for the Church of Jesus Christ of Latter-day Saints.
page 89	Tom Peters, see page 57.
page 100	Earl Fray, General Manager, EG&G.
page 127	The Quality Revolution adapted from *A New American TQM*, S. Shiba, A. Graham and D. Walden, Productivity Press, 1993, pp. 3-12.
page 151	See A New American TQM, S. Shiba, A. Graham and D. Walden, Productivity Press, 1993, p. 79 for furthur discussion.

Index to the Pearls

Problem Solving 1
   People who want milk should not seat themselves on a
        stool...in the hope a cow will back up to them . . . 2
   Fixing a problem does not necessarily prevent it from
        happening again 3
   Failing to confront fear of the unknown means living a
        life of quiet desperation. 5
   Failure is never permanent, unless you let it be 6
   The last of the human freedoms: to choose one's attitude
        in any given set of circumstances 7
   You can do nothing about the past—but you can learn
        from it 9
   Avoid blaming and embrace planning for future
        improvement 10
   Obtaining admission of guilt does not resolve problems 11
   Your reaction to your problems is your choice 12
   Owning a problem does not mean you caused the problem. 14
   Most people own more problems than necessary. 15
   Those who never accept ownership of their problems,
        never learn to solve problems 16
   You can't have vital experience without having it 17
   To help without owning the problem, listen to understand 18
   Effective listening requires suspending judgment. 19
   I can hardly wait to hear what I'm going to say next . . 21
   Separate the vital few from the trivial many 22

Influencing Without Authority 23
   Influencing should never equate with manipulating . . . 24
   To influence others *more* effectively, you must first change
        your perception of them. 25
   Choose to change your perceptions 26
   How you say something influences more than
        what you say. 27
   People respond to their perceptions in spiteof reality. 29
   Improving your influence increases your valueto an
        organization 30
   How well you communicate determines how much

influence you have	31
Winning means losing, if you are *dead* right	33
Effective communication means getting the response you want	34
The message received determines the response you get	35
People's thinking is an organization's most valuable resource	36
Clear writing forces clear thinking	37
Clear thinking enables clear communication	38
Start with the most important thing	39
K.I.S.S.: Keep It Short & Simple	41
Opinions influence more than facts	42
Complainers, even if they are right, have little influence.	43
Dumping data does not deliver a message	45
People may not care *what* you want until they understand *why*	46
The decision maker's perception is the only one that counts	47
To overcome indifference, clarify: "Why should this be considered *now*?"	48
To get action, clarify: "What if nothing is done?"	49
To win support for your ideas, reduce risk for the decision maker	50
To overcome a "no," *EMPHASIZE* the benefits.	51
Never exaggerate when trying to influence others	52
People usually respond to *minimum* expectations	53
Improvement	54
Security and stability require continuous improvement	55
Improvement always requires change	57
Change never guarantees improvement	58
Reorganizing, by itself, improves nothing	59
Getting in the groove can become a rut	60
We have met the enemy...It is us	62
All improvement lies in the process	63
Treat attitude as an *effect*, the result of experience, instead of the cause of people's behavior	64
Focus improvement on the process, not on people's attitudes	65

In business, if you stay the same, you will fall behind . 67
To focus improvement efforts on the process, assume
    everyone is trying hard and doing their best   ... 68
Do or do not. There is no try 69
There is no *instant* pudding 72
Change always costs 73
Improvement always pays 74

Managing Change 75
When will things get back to the good-old-ays?...Never 77
The goal of changing should be achieving improvement 78
We ourselves must be the change we wish to see in others 79
Managing change by compliance is easy to initiate,
    but difficult to manage 81
Managing change by commitment is difficult to initiate,
    but easy to manage 82
Start small, where you are most likely to succeed   83
People resist even the most trivial change 84
Minimize uncertainty in the transition period 85
To improve, use what you learn 87

Effective Leadership 88
Effective leaders make the right things happen 89
Traditional management versus effective leadership .. 91
Authority does not insure effective leadership 92
The most valuable skill on earth is the ability to others
    to continuously improve 93
Effective leaders *enable* continuous improvement 94
Using authority influences, but not always for
    continuous improvement 95
Malicious compliance results in everyone losing 96
Empowering does not ensure productive thinking 97
Knowing the right question is more important than
    knowing the right answers 99
To get commitment to change, failure must be tolerated. 100
Clearly define your target before trying to hit it 101
Goals + pain or gain = deceitful creative accounting ... 103
Effectiveness has higher priority than Efficiency 104
Make sure everyone pulls in the same direction 105

Meetings should focus more on effectiveness than efficiency	106
People respond to what they are held accountable for	107
To be accountable, people must have control	108

Customer Service 109

The only purpose for any job is to delight all the customers	111
Meaningful feedback from customers enables improvement	112
Your best is not good enough until all customers are delighted	113
Your enemy may be your customer	114
Keeping your eye on the goal prevents falling into activity traps	115
To delight customers, you must fully understand their needs	117
Being busy is not the same as getting results	119
Avoid this assumption: "It's clear to me, therefore, it's clear to you."	120
The customer is not always right	121
Whenever the boss is the primary customer, thinking shuts down	123
Pay particular attention to *un*realistic customer demands	124

Quality 125

Join the Quality Revolution or be overrun by it	127
Simple definition: Quality is whatever it takes to delight all the customers	128
More sophisticated definition: Quality means minimzing variation in quality characteristics	129
Dangerously wrong and woefully inadequate definition: Quality means meeting specifications	130
Quality of work determines quality of output	131
You will never be better than what is supplied	132
The quality of suppliers' work determines the quality of input	133
Total Quality involves everyone in continuous improvement	134

Controlling Quality and Service 135
  No feedback means out of control 136
  No complaints mean nothing 137
  After-the-fact measurements do not control quality . . . 139
  Authority does not control quality or service 140
  Inspection of output does not ensure future quality . . . 141
  Just because your numbers look good, does not mean
       quality and service are in control 143
  The drive-in-window approach gives no lasting
       improvement 144
  To maintain quality and service, control the work
       process 145
  If you cannot define it, you cannot control it 146
  To focus control, define quality in terms of quality
       characteristics 147
  Controlling one quality characteristic does not
       ensure control of the others 148
  Each quality characteristic requires its own work
       system 149
  Sufficiently controlling the quality of work
       guarantees quality of output 150
  The 5 Evils measure process performance 151

About The Author

Roger L. Kirkham is president of the American Training Alliance, specializing in continuous improvement training and consulting. Over the past twenty years, Mr. Kirkham has provided management and communication training for thousands of participants for clients in government, industry, and business.

He is author of the book *A Better Way: Achieving Total Quality* and has produced a four cassette, audio seminar, *Total Quality in Government, Industry & Business*. He is a licensed professional engineer and teaches part time at the University of Utah.

Mr. Kirkham is the proud father of five children, loves snow skiing and fishing in Utah, has climbed the Grand Teton in Wyoming and Mt. Fuji in Japan, and is sure that the smartest thing he ever did was marry Judy Ann Gowans.

American Training Alliance
P.O. Box 9482
Salt Lake City, UT 84109-0482
(801)521-9267; FAX (801)278-7685

*Place
First-Class
Postage
Here*

Crystal Publishing, Inc.

P.O. Box 526145
Salt Lake City, Utah 84152-6145

Yes, we'd like to order,
Please send us _____ *copies.*
Price: $6.95 per copy + shipping and handling

PEARLS OF WISDOM
for business and life

Customer Information

Mr./Mrs./Ms. _____

Title _____

Company _____

No. & Street _____

City _____

State _____ Zip+4 _____

Tel. No. ( ) _____

FAX No. _____

❑ Charge to (circle one):

VISA   MasterCard   Discover

Card No. _____ Exp. Date _____

Signature _____

Credit-card users: For your protection, please mail this card in a sealed envelope.
For faster service, call toll free 1-800-755-9777